NOAH'S ARK

ARK

Adventures on Ararat

John D. Morris

NOAH'S ARK

Adventures on Ararat

John D. Morris

Dallas, Texas
ICR.org

NOAH'S ARK
Adventures on Ararat

by John D. Morris, Ph.D.

First printing: October 2014

All Scripture quotations are from the New King James Version.

ISBN: 978-1-935587-67-5

Please visit our website for other books and resources: www.icr.org

Printed in the United States of America.

CONTENTS

PREFACE

The Flood of Noah's day was the greatest cataclysm the world has ever known. For over a year, waves of water scoured the planet, destroying everything in their path and burying millions of Earth's denizens in thick layers of mud spanning entire continents. All land creatures died—except those aboard the Ark.

The Ark, an immense barge-like ship, was built by Noah at God's command to preserve the life needed to repopulate the earth once the Flood had accomplished its judgment. After safely bringing its precious cargo through an event violent enough to reshape the planet's entire surface, it came to rest "in the seventh month, the seventeenth day of the month, on the mountains of Ararat" (Genesis 8:4). Having served its purpose, the Ark then disappeared from the Bible's pages.

But what happened to it? Over time, stories emerged of a huge, box-like object spotted on the icy slopes of Mt. Ararat in the wilds of eastern Turkey. Could it possibly be what's left of the Ark? Starting in 1972, Dr. John Morris of the Institute for Creation Research led numerous expeditions to this dangerous part of the world to find out. Here are just a few of the adventures, dangers, and difficulties he and his teams encountered.

1
WHY WE SEARCH

August, 1984

The night was absolutely jet-black. No light at all other than starlight. We were on the remote Turkish frontier in a sensitive military zone along both the Russian and Iranian borders. We were there to search the imposing Mt. Ararat for any possible remains of Noah's Ark.

Gaining permission from the Turks to search Mt. Ararat posed many problems, but we persevered. We had our permits—almost. We only lacked one signature from the local Gendarme Commander. As we waited, all we could do was pray. So around midnight, the night before we were scheduled to begin climbing, after the rest of the climbers had turned in, my co-leader and I went walking and praying, desperate for an intervention from God.

A lone Gendarme soldier appeared out of the impenetrable gloom. Screaming, shouting, and shaking, he jabbed his machine gun into my forehead and shoved me face-down in the ditch. He straddled me with his gun pointed directly at the back of my head.

He had his orders. He was trying to shoot me but had never shot a person before, and killing a man isn't easy. I shouted back as best I could in broken Turkish, but he was just an uneducated peasant from a Kurdish village and knew little Turkish.

He had been told to guard this lonely stretch of road along the militarized border, apprehend any suspicious persons, and shoot them if necessary. He had seen the alert that foreign smugglers were in the area, to be shot on sight. To him we were definitely suspicious, walking along a desolate road and speaking a language he couldn't understand. Thankfully, God answers the desperate pleas of His children, and that night, as well as on many other occasions, He answered mine.

Ararat expeditions often result in stories like mine. We've been shot at, thrown in jail, attacked by wild animals, captured by Kurdish terrorists, and robbed at gunpoint by thieves. We've endured mountaineering perils, disease, and governmental opposition. We were even struck by lightning near the summit, badly injured, and paralyzed. You might ask *Why continue the search?* What could possibly be worth all this?

Noah's Ark.

Modern and historical eyewitness accounts abound of the remains of a large boat high atop the 17,000-foot peak. Since the 1950s, Westerners have attempted to confirm them. Motivated by these reports, I traveled to Mt. Ararat over a dozen times and was subjected to some of its most severe punishment and human opposition. Yet the search goes on.

Would the Discovery of Noah's Ark Do Any Good?

Some think the Ark will never be found, that God would not allow such a discovery because people might worship it or that such obvious evidence would eliminate the need for faith. Others think the Ark has already been found. Still others, including myself, think the search should continue, following every lead—both old and new.

Regardless of the chances of finding the Ark, we can only speculate about the results of a successful search—the discovery and documentation of the Ark of Noah, compelling anyone with an open mind to deal with it. The potential good far outweighs the damage an incomplete search would have, for several reasons:

Archaeological. The great Flood of Noah's day as described in Scripture would have totally destroyed the surface of the planet. No evidence of civilization could have survived except perhaps in the form of rare artifacts. Noah's Ark constitutes the one remaining link to the pre-Flood world.

Biblical. No event in Scripture receives ridicule by scientists or doubt by skeptics as much as the Flood and Noah's Ark. Clear evidence would silence the critics of creation science and increase the faith of Christians worldwide.

Scientific. The evolution worldview invariably rests on the assumption of uniformitarianism, that "the present is the key to the past." Its basic tenet is that there has never been any episode of Earth history dramatically different from episodes possible today and that by studying the present we can come to important conclusions about the past. There is no room in this view for a supernaturally caused, mountain-covering, globally devastating flood within human history. To find the Ark atop a high mountain would destroy the concept of uniformity, the basic assumption upon which evolution rests.

Theological. Noah's Flood was a judgment on sin—that of the pre-Flood civilization. God could not and cannot allow sin to go unpunished. Noah's Ark was the means by which the few believers of that day (i.e., Noah and his family) demonstrated their faith and were saved. By calling attention to the past judgment on sin and the past Ark of safety, many minds and hearts could be focused on the coming judgment on sin and our present-day Ark of safety, Jesus Christ.

2
EYEWITNESS ACCOUNTS

As a scientist, I am unwilling to conclude the Ark is there until I see the evidence, but the eyewitness accounts of scores of individuals substantially agree with each other.[1] They describe the Ark in the same general fashion—a large, rectangular barge, usually with a catwalk and a window running its entire length. They likewise describe it as being high on the mountain but not as high as the summit. They generally claim that at the end of a long hot summer a portion of it can be seen beneath the snow and rock. Most claim it is in very steep terrain, perhaps on a ledge adjacent to a cliff. For a variety of reasons, no one has been able to pinpoint the location.

Throughout my years of searching, I compiled a brief list of eyewitness accounts.

Table of Eyewitness Accounts

1883	Turkish commissioners checking reports
WW I	Several Armenian Ararat residents
1916	Turkish soldiers returning from World War I
1916	German/Russian Weist family
1916-17	Russian expedition
1917	Russian Arutunoff had Russian photos in 1970
1930	American Mark Rafter
1935	American George Greene
1940	Australian soldiers Nice and Tibbets
1943	American soldier Ed Davis

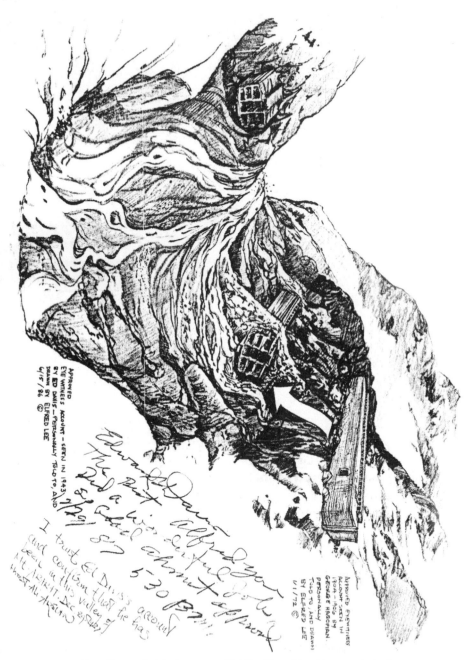

Eyewitness sketch. Image credit: Elfred Lee (Used by permission)

1943	American Vince Will
1945	American Lester Walton
1948	American airman Andy Anderson
1948	Turkish shepherd Resit
1952	American Navy photographer William Todd
1959	American Air Force George Schwinghammer
1969	American Air Force Walter Hunter
1974	American Air Force Ed Behling
1974	U.S. Navy Al Shappell
1985	Air Force General Ralph Havens
1989	U.S. Photo Interpreter George Stephen
1989	Turkish anthropologist Ahmet Arslan

The dangers of Ararat itself presented tremendous obstacles in confirming these accounts, but the political tensions in that area, as well as the suffocating amount of red tape throughout the Turkish government, made the search much more difficult.

The Ararat area had experienced almost constant war for thousands of years. Two of the ethnic groups that lived nearby caused problems, affecting the search for the Ark. The remnant of the Armenian people who lived in Russia within sight of Mt. Ararat called for retribution for the loss of their traditional homeland from which they were driven by the Turks in World War I.

The Kurdish tribes who lived on Mt. Ararat supported but did not participate in the civil war in Iraq and Syria raging over the issue of Kurdish independence. Turkey was afraid that the conflict would spread into their country. In both cases, the calling of attention to the Ararat area would have favored the causes of the minorities.

The borders of Turkey, Iran, and the former Soviet state Armenia all converged at the base of Mt. Ararat, forming a perfect storm of political turmoil. Searching for the Ark was not just an easy international flight followed by a quick hike through a beautiful countryside. It required years of dedication and the willingness to endure not just danger but frustration. Rather than climbing Mt. Ararat, most of my time in Turkey was spent driving around trying to get a permit.

Note

1. The modern-day search for the Ark had its start with Eryl and Violet Cummings' book *Noah's Ark: Fact or Fable?*, which was a compilation of eyewitness accounts published in 1973. The book spurred a generation of "ark-eologists," the name mockingly given to those who search for Noah's Ark on Mt. Ararat. I read the manuscript before it was published, and it helped turn my then-rebellious life back to Christ.

3
ROCKSLIDES AND ROBBERY

Mt. Ararat is a volcano, erupting numerous times since the Flood. Its height causes it to be covered by an ice cap that continually erodes the hardened basaltic rock underneath. As the ice sheets move along, they push the loosened rock over the edges of the mountain, causing high-speed avalanches. Often a boulder will roll like a wheel, screaming like shrapnel. On my first expedition I was warned about the "crumbly rock" but was not prepared for the enormity of the dangers it imposed.

Thursday, August 3, 1972

As we talked, I heard a noise up above us on the slope. I looked up just in time to see a rock bigger than my head hurtling through the air right at my head, traveling at great speed and only a few feet away. I ducked instantly, and it whistled by just six inches away. We stood in stunned silence for a few seconds until we saw dozens of such rocks speeding toward us from above. We left our packs and ran up the side slopes, off the glacier, and onto the loose rock. [At that point even the loose rock was safer than the glacier.] We watched as these rocks bounced all around where we had been standing, expecting to see our equipment de-molished at any second, but the shower was over within a minute and no damage had been done. We sat there

for a while, thanking God for His protection and asking for His guidance.

Once our courage returned, we stepped back onto the glacier. Again the rocks came. But we were watching for them and were up the slope before they reached us. However, one stray rock narrowly missed J.B. The situation was indeed grim. We knew the only way up that slope with such heavy packs was on the glacier. We also knew that to stay on the glacier was very dangerous. Furthermore, we knew that the Lord had called us to do a job, sent us halfway around the world, and protected us all the way. So we claimed that protection, preferring the danger to turning back.

Many more times throughout the day we were subjected to similar rock slides. The slope steepened, causing poor footing and slowing our progress, as well as making it more difficult to avoid the slides.

At one point, the side slope that provided us some protection dwindled down to very little. I raced up this small slope once to avoid a slide, but the rocks continued to fall all around me. I ripped off my pack, threw it down, and began dodging, running, jumping, falling, and praying, trying to avoid the rocks. It's very hard to be nimble-footed on these loose rock slopes, especially when wearing metal crampons. But the Lord was in complete control, and I escaped without a scratch, even though many large rocks passed within inches.

The rocks vary from walnut size to Volkswagen size, but at such dizzying speeds even the small ones could kill. We developed a keen awareness of rock slides weeks earlier in the Ahora Gorge, but these slides were vastly different. They make very little noise in the snow but fall with such force that they shake the earth. The speeds probably reach 100 mph. Their bounces are unpredictable, and it is hard to get out of their way. As they fall, they fly through the air sometimes for hundreds of feet, spinning like a wheel and whistling like shrapnel. Each rock is like a buzz saw and would destroy anything in its path, but we felt we were in the Lord's will and continued climbing the slope.

There were, of course, other dangers on Ararat. The packs of Kurdish wolfhounds that prowled around the mountain were vicious, bigger than German shepherds, and ugly.

During my first expedition, I was climbing in the Ahora Gorge when my coworker and I were surrounded and attacked by more than ten of these wolfhounds. We each had a rock in our hands and tried to scare the dogs away, but the

I learned years later that the technical name for the Kurdish wolfhound is the Anatolian Shepherd.

pack closed in—like wolves. Several drooled and foamed at the mouth. They were ready for blood.

Thankfully, the Lord demonstrated His providence, and a Kurdish shepherd showed up and started beating them with a stick. Apparently, three of the dogs were his own. With a brief "thanks" to the stranger, we started off at a fast walk, thanking God for His protection.

The following events on Ararat happened to the climbers in my group, and I recorded them in my diary. There were five of us on this trip in 1972, and at one time we split up. Two of us went one way, and the other three (Roger, Skip, and Bill) went another way, carrying most of our gear. The three of them were traveling with a family of Kurdish shepherds and camped for the night at the foot of a glacier.

Saturday, August 12, 1972

> Late that night, they were awakened by the sound of a nearby gunshot. They heard several people moving outside and then a whole volley of shots rang out, followed by much shouting and more shots. Roger sat up and shouted back that they had permission from their friends in the Gendarme to climb, but as he talked a bullet ripped through the tent, narrowly missing his head. He shouted for them to stop and crawled out. Immediately three men surrounded him, jabbing him with their gun barrels and hitting him with clubs while shining a flashlight in his face. Skip and Bill followed and received the same treatment. As they were herded out onto the rocks, all three felt that they were going to be killed.
>
> One of the men, an older man, was extremely harsh and cruel, and as he appeared to be preparing to kill them, Skip and Roger and Bill prayed for him and the others because it was obvious that Satan was in control of their lives and they needed Jesus Christ and His salvation desperately. One of the thieves was moved

by this and restrained the older man from shooting and from any more harsh treatment. He guarded the three climbers while the older man and the third man cleaned out the tent, taking everything they could carry. When the thieves left, the only things they left behind were the sleeping bags, the tent, the ice axes, and the boots. These things were the only things necessary for survival and retreat back down the mountain. Nothing could be done that night, so the three men went back to sleep.

The value of the stolen gear was about $3,000, and that was over 40 years ago. We reported the robbery to a Turkish commander, who promised to look for the gear and bring the thieves to justice. However, we had little hope this would happen.

When we left Turkey, we were satisfied that the loss of our equipment had been allowed by God and that we would never see it again. But as God's providence would have it, three months later, the night before Thanksgiving, our gear was delivered to my house.

4

LIGHTNING STRIKES

Thursday, August 3, 1972
Near the summit of Mt. Ararat

The snow was falling harder....sliding down the slope, covering our knees at all times. The wind was blowing hard, and it was difficult to see. We stopped under a big rock, providing us a little shelter from the wind, and since the time was 1:00, we broke out our trail food. As we ate, Roger dropped his sunglasses, and they fell down a hole at his feet. As he reached his hand down after them, he discovered that the hole went on forever. Come to find out, we were standing on a thin ice covering over a large crevasse where the rock and ice separated. Needless to say, we moved.

Since the snow was coming down in such torrents, and we were on the steepest part of the glacier, we decided to rope up, cross the finger glacier to the other side, and continue our ascent on the rocky-side slope. The rocks were almost completely covered with freshly fallen snow and were much more stable than before.

We got the feeling that we were right in the middle of a war. It seemed that Satan was doing his best to destroy us, and God was protecting....I had felt that this day we would find the Ark....[It felt as if Satan] was desperately trying to stop us...such a discovery would have [a tremendous impact] on the world. But we were filled with a real peace, knowing that no matter how tough the going got, the Lord was protecting and leading, and nothing could happen unless the Lord allowed it to happen. We were in His will and on His mission, and whatever happened we knew [it] would be according to His purpose. How wonderful it is to be a Christian and know that you are right where God wants you.

The weather got worse. The temperature dropped, the wind blew harder, and the snow got thicker. We were on a slope of about 45° and only 100 feet below the ridge or shoulder of the mountain where we had planned to make camp, when thunder clapped all around us and lightning struck nearby. Lightning began striking all around. Every large rock in the area was struck repeatedly.

This was the first time I was ever in a storm—I mean IN a storm. We were actually in the clouds. Lightning was not striking in bolts, it was just collecting at one place or another. The thunder was deafening all around us. Static electricity was evident everywhere. Our ice axes and crampons were singing, our hair was standing on end, even J.B.'s beard and my moustache were sticking straight out. We could feel the electricity build up until it collected on some nearby rock.

In our training, we had been taught to avoid electrical storms if at all possible, but if ever caught in one to try and stay away from large rocks. The storm had come up quickly, and we were surrounded by big rocks and just below the ridge of huge rocks. Our only hope of safety was to continue upwards over the ridge of rocks and onto the relatively flat glacier, staying close enough to big rocks so that we ourselves would not be struck directly.

Although we were in a most dangerous situation, I felt that we would not be struck. I knew that Satan was again trying to stop us and that God was allowing the storm but protecting us, and that if we kept our faith in Him, with His help we would overcome the situation.

The wind and snow kept increasing as we neared the top. At one point, J.B. sat down beneath a large rock to rest and gain some relief from the blinding snow. I had seen lightning strike this rock several times and returned to warn him....[It was no use yelling through the wind and snow, so we took the risk and went to J.B.]... but as all three of us stood or sat on this big rock, lightning struck it again, sending unbelievable bolts of electricity through us.

J.B. was frozen to the rock by his back. His arms and legs and head were extended out into the air. He was in no pain at that time even though he could feel electricity surging through his body. From that vantage point, however, he could see Roger and me thrown off the rock. The force of the lightning seemed to suspend us in the air and then dropped us far down the slope. At this point, J.B. succeeded in forcing one of his legs to the ground, completing the electrical circuit, and the force somersaulted him down the mountain, following Roger and me.

I had been standing on the rock (now known as "Zap Rock") when the lightning struck. Once again I had been thanking the Lord for protecting us, feeling that we would not be harmed. When the bolt struck, my whole body went numb, and I could not see or move but never lost consciousness. I fell over backwards, still wearing my heavy pack. I expected an impact, but it never came; it seemed like I was floating very slowly for several seconds. I was gently lain on the snow by unseen hands and began sliding down the steep slope. I knew I must stop, and for an instant my eyes and arms would not function. When they did, I spied and grabbed a [boulder] in the snow, stopping my slide.

For a few seconds I lay there, not moving, aware only of intense pain. I reasoned that since the pain was so great that I had received the full force of the bolt and that the other two [men] were unaffected. I tried to roll over and sit up, but to my horror found that both legs were paralyzed. There was no sensation of touch or life in them, just burning, searing pain.

I called to my friends for help, thinking they were unharmed, but the only answer was another call for help. Looking back uphill, I saw J.B. sitting up in the snow, about ten feet away, obviously also in great pain, with one leg twisted underneath him. He also was paralyzed and thought the one leg was broken.

We remained there for some minutes, crying out to God for relief from the pain and deliverance from the horrible death that surely was to be ours. Suddenly I missed Roger and called to him, frantically looking around for him. J.B. spotted him much farther down the mountain, lying face down in the snow, one side of his head covered with blood. We were unable to go to him but prayed for him and called to him from above. Finally, he stood up, looked around, and walked up to us. His face was at least as white as the snow, and his eyes were filled with confusion and fear. He did not come all the way to J.B. and me but, from a few feet away, bombarded us with questions. "Where are we? What are we doing here? Why don't we go sit under that big rock and get out of this snow?" J.B. patiently tried to explain to him that we were on Mt. Ararat, looking for Noah's Ark, and had just been struck by lightning under that big rock.

Roger was in shock and experiencing total amnesia. He didn't know who he was, who we were, he didn't know anything; furthermore, he didn't even like us. He wondered who these two nuts were sitting in the snow, freezing to death, when they could gain some shelter from the storm up among the rocks. J.B. convinced him to go get our ice axes, but that was the only thing he would do to help.

So J.B. and I, unable to help ourselves, had to rely totally upon God. We reasoned that Roger would slip into deep shock soon and would need medical attention. J.B. thought his leg was broken, and both of us were paralyzed, unable to move. We discussed the possible descent of the mountain but ruled it out as impossible.

Our situation was, in short, critical. Unless we were able to get to some shelter, we would die within a few hours, freezing to death in the storm. And so, not being able to see any way to alter the situation, I prepared to die.

That's a weird feeling, rationally knowing that you are about to die. I never once doubted my salvation and did not fear death. In fact, I felt real peace, knowing that soon I was to be with my Savior in heaven. I had always envisioned meeting Jesus face to face as a rather exciting experience, but I now felt no excitement, just comfort. In fact, I wanted to get on with it — to die now, rather than slowly over a period of hours.

As I sat there, contemplating the horrible death in store, the Holy Spirit began to interject some of His thoughts into my mind. First, I was reminded of the hundreds of thousands of Christians who have suffered and died while following the Lord's leading and how they considered it a privilege to suffer for Him. Then I was reminded of the marvelous way in which our group had been led in the past months and particularly the past weeks in Turkey. I was reminded of the miraculous ac-quisition of our VW minibus, of the Christian friends who

had helped us, of the granting of the impossible permits, of all the many dead-end streets down which we
had wandered only to find an open door at the end. I was
reminded of the Christians back home who were praying
for our safety and success. I was reminded of the job
we had been called to do and its implications, importance,
and urgency.

And then the conclusion! No, I wasn't going to die. God
still had a purpose, a job for us to accomplish. He
wasn't going to let us die up in that frozen wasteland.
Somehow, He was going to remedy the situation, heal
and strengthen our bodies, and allow us to continue the
search for the Ark.

I was reminded of two passages of Scripture: James 5:15
which states that, "The prayer of faith will save
the sick," and 1 John 5:14-15 stating that, "This is the
confidence that we have in Him, that if we ask anything
according to His will, He hears us. And if we know that
He hears us, whatever we ask, we know that we have
the petitions that we have asked of Him."

These thoughts were all whirling around in my head at
dizzying speeds. I knew I wasn't going to die. I knew that
I was going to be healed. I knew that this was according
to God's will. And since I knew these things would come
to pass, and if I had that faith, then I could pray the
prayer of faith. And so, with my heart pounding wildly,
I prayed that prayer of faith, knowing that the Lord
heard me and knowing that He would answer my request
and heal my body.

Before the Holy Spirit had directed my thinking, I had
prayed for relief from the pain and for healing. But it

was a prayer of desperation not of faith. This time
I expected a miracle. I tried to move my legs—no
response. Or did that toe move? Frantically I began
massaging my legs and could feel the firmness return.
There was no sensation of touch in them, just a burning
numbness. Before when I had felt them, they resembled
a balloon filled with water, shapeless and pliable. But
now they were hard. I continued to massage, covering
them with snow to ease the burning sensation. Their
strength gradually returned, but still no feeling. Within
thirty minutes, my knees would bend! Within an hour, I
could stand!

Using an ice axe as a cane, I hobbled over to J.B. and
massaged his legs. He had been unable to reach his
ankle and still thought it was broken. We determined
that it was not broken, but both legs felt like jelly. He
was quite calm and relaxed and felt that Roger needed
attention more than he.

Roger was sitting on a nearby rock, obviously cold and
still in shock. He didn't even have the sense to put
on heavier clothing. So I retrieved his pack and re-
dressed him—nylon pants, down parka, wind parka, and
poncho. As I was tying his poncho up around his chin, a
look of recognition crossed his face, and his memory
began to return. When he asked why I was dressing
him, I knew he was going to be all right. He did not fully
recover for several hours but in the meantime was able
to heat some water for a hot drink. In doing so, we lost
all of the coffee, cocoa, tea, soup, all hot drink material.
It slid down the hill, along with some valuable equipment.

J.B. had been massaging and flexing his legs all this

time. His right leg had recuperated somewhat, and he could move it. Roger and I helped him...don warmer clothing and find shelter from the storm.

Finally, I began to dress myself. My legs were weak and shaky. I had walked up and down the slope, gathering gear, until [I was] exhausted; but together we huddled under the rock to gain shelter from the storm...and prayed to gain victory over the situation.

Earlier, the Holy Spirit had given me the knowledge that it was in the Lord's will for us to be healed and to survive the ordeal. Now we were partially healed and growing stronger each minute, but we still faced a cruel blizzard with little chance of survival. Lightning was still flashing everywhere, snow was still coming down in buckets, and gale winds were blowing. We knew we were going to survive but that it wouldn't be easy.

We, as Christians, are expected to have faith, large amounts of it in fact; but we must never expect our faith to be sufficient. Frequently the Lord requires hard work and then rewards our faith by blessing our efforts. Such was the case on the mountain. [We thought the] only possible area of safety was on top of the ridge away from the big rocks. We needed a flat place to pitch the tent...[to get out of] the storm, so as soon as the lightning intensity lessened, Roger and I began searching for a way to the top.

The wind was blowing the snow so hard we could not see more than 10 feet maximum, but we located a path between several huge rocks and climbed it. It was nearly vertical and footing was treacherous. Once we reached the top, however, we found the weather worse. We were right on the edge of [a major glacier], and the wind velocity doubled, but we picked out a flat place to camp and returned to J.B.

J.B. had been massaging and exercising his legs. His right leg had regained its strength, but [he had] no response from his left. He still could not move, so Roger and I climbed the slope with our packs and made plans to anchor the rope to a rock and assist J.B. in his ascent. I was nearly exhausted after this second climb. My legs were shaking like rubber, so I rested in the snow for several minutes. We descended once again to J.B., and much to our surprise found him standing up, waiting for us. His legs still had no feeling, but their strength had returned enough to allow him to stand, so Roger carried his pack and with [a] little assistance from me J.B. climbed that vertical slope on two numb, weak legs!

Within minutes of the time we reached the top, the storm broke. I guess the Lord figured that we had had enough. The snow and wind stopped, and the clouds disappeared just as suddenly as they had appeared. In complete comfort and peace, we were able to pitch our tent and eat a hot supper. In fact, that evening before the sun went down, it was rather warm and pleasant.

Throughout the day...I had felt that this would be the day we would find the Ark. This feeling was strengthened by the fact that Satan was so determined to stop us. It's not hard to imagine what I was doing and thinking as we pitched the tent and set up camp. As soon as time permitted, I wandered off to the edge of the Ahora Gorge, positive that the Ark was in full view. I did not approach any dangerous cliffs but with binoculars

searched in all directions from a safe vantage point.
Much to my disappointment, I did not see the Ark, but
the view of the gorge from above was magnificent. The
freshly fallen snow covered everything above elevation
9,000 feet, including, I suspected, the Ark. So we had to
settle for a comfortable place to sleep, hot food, and
our lives that night. We were satisfied and gave thanks
to God. Very few people have ever camped that high on
Ararat, but I'm sure no one else has had such a wonderful time of prayer and singing as we had that evening.

5
ARCHAEOLOGICAL DISCOVERIES

We never found the Ark. While this is disappointing, the discoveries we made along the way added to our knowledge of the history of Ararat that, in addition to a few good stories, at least made our scientific efforts worthwhile.

On multiple expeditions, we investigated a cave in some cliffs near an ancient abandoned fortress. Two men with turbans and staffs were carved on either side of its entrance. Above the entrance a four-legged animal was carved, but its head had eroded beyond recognition. Scholars studied these carvings to determine that the cave was from a civilization older than the Hittites. We went down a staircase to a foyer-looking area where we saw the remains of what appeared to be a coffin. The walls of the cave were very smooth—someone had spent a lot of time carving them.

In 1972, we visited the area of Korhan, an ancient site of worship. Near the top of a foothill, a large rock was discovered. It was covered with both pictorial writing and an ancient style of cuneiform, more pictorial in form than Sumerian cuneiform and even more ancient. Many other structures and remains were located, which seemingly had not been noticed before. Surrounding the altar at the very summit of the hill were approximately 25 sacrificial pits, which were used perhaps by later civilizations or lesser personages than those who used the main superbly constructed one. An ancient graveyard was located nearby with ornate carvings and crosses on the tombstones. Either a large washbasin or a key-base for a statue was nearby. Down at the foot of the hill was an Armenian graveyard with perhaps 30 to 50 ornate tombstones. Crosses and carvings were also discovered on the walls of the huge shrine at the base of the hill. Was this a civilization of Noah's early descendants?

In 1984, a group announced to the world that they had found Noah's Ark. Years later, someone even wrote a book about it. My team and I happened to be at Ararat during this announcement, but we did not get excited. It was generally known among "ark-eologists" that the object they were talking about was just an unusual rock several miles south of the mountain, but we investigated anyway just in case the news reporters asked us why we disagreed.

As expected, it was just a formation of rock. The general shape had been eroded by mudslides. We found fragments that would certainly appear to be petrified

wood—to an amateur. It's not unusual for people to make these kinds of claims about the location of the Ark.

The cave and artifacts mentioned here were formed by ancient inhabitants near where the Ark might have landed. Perhaps someday they can be examined more closely so we can learn more about the early civilizations that sprang up after the Flood.

6
THE SEARCH GOES ON

The truth of the great Flood of Noah's day can never be forgotten. We encounter the evidence everywhere we go. We encounter evidence of it every time we study or even see nature. We are forced to ponder the ways of God when we look at the remains of the Flood, like rocks and fossils. He revealed the truth of creation and the Flood, complete with news of His holy nature. God hates sin—always has and always will. He has declared the ultimate penalty for sin to be death. And He is not the sort of God to let sin go unpunished. We know that we are sinners who have broken His law numerous times and are ourselves under His righteous death penalty.

We can do nothing to alter this fact any more than someone in Noah's day, simply by disbelieving Noah's proclamation that the great Flood was coming, could have altered the fact and stopped the Flood from coming. The Flood came anyway, just as God's judgment is coming. In fact, Jesus Christ Himself compared the coming judgment by fire to the past judgment by water (Matthew 24:37-39). No one will escape.

But just as in Noah's day, He provides a way of escape to those who believe. Noah and his family were saved. Everyone else perished. In our case, God has provided His only Son, our Lord and Savior Jesus Christ. He came to Earth as a man, a sinless man who had no death penalty of His own to pay. By so doing, He was qualified to die for me and you. He died as a sacrifice so that we wouldn't have to die. We must simply believe that He died in our place, offering us forgiveness of our sins. And then He rose from the grave, having conquered death, offering us eternal life.

The Ark account is then of ultimate importance to us. Just as the believers in that day had to get on board the Ark for safety, so we must accept God's free gift of forgiveness and eternal life through the work of Jesus Christ on the cross by believing that it applies to me.

Settle it forever with Him. Come to Him in faith, and He will respond with forgiveness, adoption into His family, and eternal life.

It may be that as a symbol of that salvation, the Ark still rests somewhere on Mt. Ararat. Many expeditions over the years, including mine, have attempted to find it, but none so far have been definitively successful. Perhaps God will never allow it to be found. We may never know. Until then, the search continues for the Ark—the last remaining link to the "world that then existed" (2 Peter 3:6).

ABOUT THE AUTHOR

Between 1972 and 1989, Dr. John Morris traveled to Turkey over a dozen times to look for Noah's Ark. The search for the Ark marked a turning point in his life. He was an engineer in Los Angeles and living a defeated Christian life when he turned back to God and dedicated himself to sharing biblical truth, eventually earning a Ph.D. in geological engineering and joining the Institute for Creation Research. In his many Ararat expeditions, he witnessed abundant answers to prayer, especially preservation in times of mortal danger. He never found what he was looking for, but he and his team members did discover more about God, His nature, His power, and how they could fit into His plan. Much of Dr. Morris' experience in searching for the Ark is recorded in *Adventure on Ararat, Noah's Ark and the Ararat Adventure, The Ark on Ararat* (co-authored with Dr. Tim LaHaye), articles, and presentations.

Some of his best contributions to the field of creation science have been *The Young Earth, The Fossil Record*, and *The Global Flood*. Drawing on Dr. Morris' extensive knowledge of geology and paleontology, these books present solid scientific evidences in support of the Genesis narrative. In them, he not only demonstrates the scientific accuracy of the Bible but also brings glory to God by showing the wonders of His creation.

Dr. Morris no longer climbs mountains or fights wild dogs, and so the search is passed on to a new generation. But the Ark still compels him, and he supports and encourages those who take up the creation cause—and he does it with the same kindness and compassion that have been staples of his character.

An Enduring Message

At ICR today, the team of scientists, scholars, and staff continues with the work of creation ministry, and ICR's message remains steady— God is faithful and His Word is true. We can be confident that true science confirms the accuracy of Scripture. And we can trust Him with the details of life—those seen and those yet to be revealed, including the biblical account of Noah's Ark.

Whether or not the Ark is ever found, there is abundant evidence of the truth of God's Word. "For since the creation of the world His invisible attributes are clearly seen, being understood by the things that are made, even His eternal power and Godhead" (Romans 1:20).

For over four decades, the Institute of Creation Research has been making "clearly seen" the truths of the Bible. And ICR will continue doing what Dr. John Morris and others before and after him have done so well: Proclaiming scientific truth in creation.

Endnote: Some of the journal entries were adapted from Dr. John Morris' *Adventure on Ararat*, Institute for Creation Research, 1973.

APPENDIX

Application Letter for the 1972 Expedition to Mt. Ararat

In the months preceding the Institute for Creation Research's expedition to Mt. Ararat in 1972, many qualified and concerned individuals contacted me and asked to be included in the search. Frequently I prayed diligently over each applicant and wrote a short letter or called to inform these men that the Lord did not seem to indicate that they were the right ones for the job. But there were three men to whom I wrote the following letter. These three men had the right qualifications, and the more we prayed about them the clearer it became that these were the men whom God had chosen to continue the search for the remains of Noah's Ark.

Dear _____,

Thank you for your letter indicating your interest in joining our Ararat expedition. We are still in need of men to join us in the search, but have made it a matter of real prayer that the Lord make known His will to us and that the right group of men will be drawn together.

Before any decision is made concerning your personal involvement, I would like to acquaint you with our specific plans and also the dangers involved. If, after reading this letter and seeking God's will, you still feel led to join us, contact me or my second-in-command, John Seiter, at this same address.

To begin with, each member of the team will be required to undergo a week of intensive training on Mt. Hood, near Portland, Oregon, to master the techniques of glacial travel, rescue, and survival. This training is scheduled for the middle of June.

While I have no doubt that you are physically fit and can successfully climb Mt. Ararat, I want to make sure that you realize the dangers and hardships involved. For the most part, we will be on or just below a glacier, the permanent icecap of the mountain. Problems with crevasses, landslides, rockslides, and blizzards will be everyday occurrences. When not on the glacier itself, we will be traveling through and sleeping in the territory of the Kurds. The Kurds live on the slopes of the mountain and are subject to no formal legal system. Some of them are also capable of slitting one's throat as he sleeps. The Turkish Army, which patrols the area, will not allow us to continue the search if we are suspected of any anti-Turkish activities, since Mt. Ararat is near the border of Turkey and Russia. Some people have been shot instantly in such situations, and others arrested for spying.

My point is this—this endeavor should not be confused with a romantic adventure. There is a real possibility of injury and even death. In fact, the obstacles are so numerous that a successful search would be impossible without the help of God.

Concerning finances, each member of the team is responsible for paying his own way. No general appeal for money has been made, simply because we want to remain inconspicuous. Several people have donated money throughout the past few months, and it will be used for needs that concern the entire group. The personal cost for each person will be $2,000.

Dedication to the task of finding the Ark is a prime requirement and is an overriding issue in the selection of personnel. Of the five-man team, only three will be together on the upper reaches of the mountain at any time. These three, however, will have to climb the treacherous slopes with up to a 75-pound pack on their backs, endure extreme weather conditions, eat lukewarm dehydrated food, and sleep in a crawl-in tent for a week at a time. Each member must be willing to take orders and submit to the leader's direction. There will be no room for arguments, bickering, and insubordination.

Upon returning to the States, it is hoped that we will have the chance to share our experiences with interested churches and schools. Our purpose in finding the Ark is not to gain wealth or fame but to win souls for Jesus Christ, and our hope is that the evidence we bring back will cause many people to believe God's Word. It is likely that many churches and Christian groups will desire speakers who were directly involved with the discovery of the Ark to come and share their experiences and findings with them. We have an obligation to God to use this opportunity to further His kingdom here on Earth. If this is not your goal and desire as a Christian, then you should not consider joining our group.

Let me summarize the requirements for prospective personnel in order of their importance, as I see them:

1. Theology—Be sound in conservative Christian doctrine and have a deep desire to see people come to know Jesus Christ as their Lord and Savior.

2. Dedication—Have a willingness to risk life and health to find Noah's Ark because of its evangelical implications.

3. Personality—Have a personality that is harmonious with the others in the group and a determination to maintain goodwill and peace.

4. Speaking Ability—Possess the means and desire to tell others of the meaning of Noah's Ark.

5. Physical Ability—Have the physical strength and endurance needed to climb one of the highest mountains in the world.

6. Financial Backing—The ability to pay one's own way or to raise the support without any commitments to non-Christian organizations.

I have tried to portray to you in this letter just what to expect in regard to our trip. I have been as honest and straightforward as possible. I want to make sure that you know what is involved before you reaffirm your desire to join our group. I think you should talk it over with your family and diligently seek God's will before making a decision.

Please write me and tell me more about yourself, your religious background and Christian life, your personal dedication to this cause, and your thoughts about the trip. We have prayed daily that the Lord will provide the right men for the job, and if He has spoken to you in this matter, please let me know.

Yours for the Ark,

John D. Morris